ROBOTS EXPLORING SPACE

MARS PROBES

Robots Explore the Red Planet

Kelly Spence

PowerKiDS press™

NEW YORK

Published in 2017 by **The Rosen Publishing Group**
29 East 21st Street, New York, NY 10010

Produced for Rosen by Calcium

Editors for Calcium: Sarah Eason and Harriet McGregor
Designers for Calcium: Jennie Child
Picture researcher: Rachel Blount

Picture credits: Cover: NASA/JPL-Caltech/University Arizona (Mars Probe image),Thinkstock:
Pixtum (top banner), Shutterstock: Andrey_Kuzmin (metal plate), Thinkstock: -strizh- (back cover
illustration); Inside: CNES: ESA 26; NASA: 6, 21, JPL-Caltech 9, 11, 19, 25, JPL/Corby Waste 5, Pat
Rawlings, SAIC 29; Wikimedia Commons: NASA/JPL 23, NASA/JPL/Corby Waste 16, NASA/JPL-
Caltech/Cornell 12-13, NASA/JPL-Caltech/MSSS/NMMNHS 15.

CATALOGING-IN-PUBLICATION DATA

Names: Spence, Kelly.
Title: Mars probes: robots explore the red planet / Kelly Spence.
Description: New York : Powerkids Press, 2017. | Series: Robots exploring space | Includes index.
Identifiers: ISBN 9781508151326 (pbk.) | ISBN 9781508151265 (library bound) |
   ISBN 9781508151159 (6 pack)
Subjects: LCSH: Mars (Planet)--Juvenile literature. | Mars probes--Juvenile literature.
Classification: LCC QB641.S73 2017 | DDC 523.43--dc23

Manufactured in the United States of America
CPSIA Compliance Information: Batch #BS16PK. For Further Information contact Rosen Publishing, New York, New York at 1-800-237-9932

CONTENTS

The Red Planet

For hundreds of years, Mars has fascinated humans. The planet is visible to the naked eye, shining like a star with a reddish glow in the night sky. Many questions have been asked about the red planet: Has there ever been life on Mars? Has there ever been liquid water on the planet's surface? Could humans survive there? Robotic exploration is helping scientists find the answers to these questions and many more.

Robots to Mars

So far, **robots** have been the only travelers from Earth to reach Mars. Missions to the red planet have taken place in three stages: **flybys, orbiters**, and landers and rovers. A flyby consists of sending a spacecraft on a one-way trip past a planet or moon. An orbiter is designed to cycle around the planet in a curved path, studying Mars from the sky. Landers and rovers are **probes** that have touched down on the Martian surface.

Making Mars on Earth

Space agencies spend billions of dollars sending robots to Mars. Facilities such as the Mars Yard, located at the Jet Propulsion Lab (JPL) in California, allow scientists to recreate the Martian surface. Rocks, sand, and other obstacles just like those found on the surface of Mars give scientists the chance to test-drive rovers and study different scenarios before they send instructions to the robotic explorers on Mars. One mistake can have serious consequences when robots are traveling millions of miles away.

This artwork shows the *Mars Global Surveyor (MGS)* orbiting above the Martian atmosphere.

SPACE DISCOVERY

HUMANS HAVE OBSERVED MARS FOR CENTURIES. THE FAMOUS POLISH ASTRONOMER NICOLAUS COPERNICUS (1473–1543) WAS THE FIRST TO PROPOSE THAT MARS WAS A DISTANT PLANET. ANOTHER ASTRONOMER, GALILEO GALILEI (1564–1642), WAS THE FIRST PERSON TO VIEW MARS THROUGH A TELESCOPE.

The Mariner Missions

The *Mariner* program was the first program set up by the National Aeronautics and Space Administration (NASA) to explore the three inner planets found near Earth: Mercury, Venus, and Mars.

Mariner 3 and *Mariner 4* were the first robots destined for the red planet. Each spacecraft was fitted with a camera that could take about 20 photos. *Mariner 3* launched November 5, 1964. Shortly after takeoff, the protective casing around *Mariner 3* failed to open. This blocked the **solar panels** and kept them from charging. As a result, the spacecraft soon ran out of fuel.

Mariner 3 weighed in at 575 pounds (261 kg).

All hope was now on *Mariner 4* and just a few weeks later, on November 28, the robot began its one-way journey. The mission had one shot at traveling past Mars at just the right angle. On July 14, 1965, *Mariner 4* reached its destination. It beamed back the first pictures using the Deep Space Network (DSN). Four days later these images reached **mission control**, arriving as **binary code** that was then made into a picture by a computer.

Mapping the Red Planet

Two years later, NASA sent another team of spacecraft to fly by Mars, *Mariner 6* and *Mariner 7*. These missions were followed by *Mariner 9*. This flying robot was designed to orbit Mars. This would allow scientists to study the planet over a much longer period of time.

When the spacecraft arrived, a storm was raging on the planet below. NASA instructed the robot to wait for the storm to end before it began taking pictures of the planet's surface. For about a year, *Mariner 9* mapped the entire Martian surface, showing ancient riverbeds, an enormous canyon, and massive volcanoes. It also captured the first closeup shots of Mars's two moons, Phobos and Deimos. *Mariner 9* sent its last message on October 27, 1972, bringing an end to the first program to explore Mars.

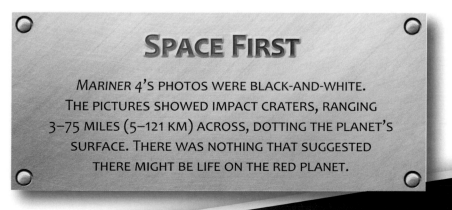

SPACE FIRST

MARINER 4'S PHOTOS WERE BLACK-AND-WHITE. THE PICTURES SHOWED IMPACT CRATERS, RANGING 3–75 MILES (5–121 KM) ACROSS, DOTTING THE PLANET'S SURFACE. THERE WAS NOTHING THAT SUGGESTED THERE MIGHT BE LIFE ON THE RED PLANET.

Viking 1 and 2

The *Viking* missions marked the next step forward in Mars exploration. This time, NASA was sending two robots to the planet's surface.

Arriving at Mars

Viking 1 and *Viking 2* were each made up of two important parts: an orbiter and a lander. *Viking 1* launched on August 20, 1975, with *Viking 2* following on September 9. Each orbiter-lander made the year-long trip to Mars together. Upon arrival, the orbiters began taking photos of the planet below. Using these pictures, scientists decided that their original landing sites for the landers were not safe. Two new sites were chosen. *Lander 1* touched down on July 20, 1976, on the western side of Chryse Planitia (the Plains of Gold). *Lander 2* set down at Utopia Planitia on September 3.

Did *Viking* Find Life?

The robots conducted the first science experiments on another planet. *Viking 1* used its robotic arm to scoop up soil to be placed in its onboard laboratory for testing. These tests were searching for signs of life, hiding in the rocky surface. While the *Viking* mission

SPACE FIRST

VIKING 1 EARNED ITS PLACE IN HISTORY AS THE FIRST HUMAN-MADE SPACECRAFT TO SUCCESSFULLY TOUCH DOWN ON MARS. THE TWIN LANDERS ALSO TOOK THE FIRST CLOSEUP PICTURES OF THE PLANET'S DUSTY SURFACE.

This artwork of the *Viking* lander shows its long arm scooping up soil for analysis.

did not find life on Mars, the experiments they conducted did detect ingredients that could support life. More than 30 years later, scientists have carried out a new analysis of the *Viking* data. Today, they believe that *Viking* might have found signs of life after all.

Both landers were powered by plutonium, a radioactive **element** that releases energy as it breaks down. *Lander 2* remained operational until 1980. *Lander 1* continued to send data back to Earth for another two years afterward.

Science from the Sky

The orbiters took pictures of geologic formations that supported the theory that liquid water had existed on Mars. *Orbiter 1* also flew within 56 miles (90 km) of Phobos, Mars's largest moon. On July 25, 1978, *Orbiter 2* ran out of fuel. NASA scientists made adjustments to conserve enough fuel to power *Orbiter 1* for another two years.

Pathfinder and Sojourner

The Mars *Pathfinder* mission was the first in history to send a free-ranging rover to the red planet. The rover, named *Sojourner* after Sojourner Truth (c. 1797–1883), the U.S. civil rights hero, caught a ride aboard a lander taking off on December 4, 1996.

Built to Drive

Sojourner was tiny. The rover weighed just under 25 pounds (11 kg) and was powered by solar panels attached to its back. For the rocky Martian ground, the six-wheeled explorer used a rocker-bogie system that allowed each wheel to turn independently. Motion sensors in *Sojourner*'s frame warned the robot, and its operators, if there was a danger of it tipping over.

Bumpy Landing

The spacecraft successfully reached the planet surface on July 1, 1997, using a parachute and airbags to land. The landing site was Ares Vallis, a plain littered with rocks. Once *Pathfinder* was on the ground, *Sojourner* rolled down the launch ramp. It was time for the little robot to go for a spin.

Driving Solo

Not all of *Sojourner*'s trek was steered remotely. The coordinates for specific sites were sent to the rover, but then it was up to *Sojourner* to use its "brains" to **autonomously** drive itself there. The onboard

Sojourner (front) marked the first generation of robotic rovers to visit Mars.

computer used sophisticated software to examine pictures of the surrounding area, on the lookout for dangerous obstacles. It would then decide on the safest route, which *Sojourner* followed to its destination.

During the mission the little robot did not go far. *Sojourner* only traveled up to 40 feet (12 m) away from *Pathfinder*. *Sojourner* took 550 photos and *Pathfinder* snapped more than 16,500. The successful mission paved the way for a future generation of rovers to explore the red planet.

SPACE DISCOVERY

ONCE SOJOURNER REACHED ITS TARGET, A SPECTROMETER WAS USED TO ANALYZE THE BASIC ELEMENTS THAT MADE UP THE ROCK. DURING THE MISSION, SOJOURNER CONDUCTED TESTS ON 15 DIFFERENT ROCKS AND WAS ABLE TO CONFIRM THAT VOLCANIC ACTIVITY ONCE TOOK PLACE ON MARS. NASA SCIENTISTS HAVE GIVEN THESE ROCKS UNIQUE NAMES, SUCH AS YOGI AND BARNACLE BILL.

Spirit

All planets travel on different paths around the sun. Scientists knew that in 2003, Mars would be closer to Earth than it had been for thousands of years. It was the perfect opportunity to launch a new Mars mission. Twin rovers, *Spirit* and *Curiosity*, were destined for the red planet.

Geologists on Wheels

The rovers were designed for a 90-**sol** mission, with geology as their main focus. Each robotic geologist had five instruments aboard to study the rocks and soil of Mars. Nine different cameras acted as the robot's eyesight. One camera was positioned to record images 5 feet and 2 inches (1.6 m) off the ground. This gives scientists an idea of what the planet would look like if a human were standing there. The rovers first sent their data to the Mars *Odyssey* orbiter, which then beamed their data back to Earth.

Dust Devils

Although both robots carried batteries as backup power, solar panels were the main power source for each rover. *Spirit* was the first rover to observe spinning clouds of loose particles, called dust devils, forming on Mars. Scientists believe that these dust devils helped both *Spirit* and *Opportunity* outlive their planned mission length. When a swirling cloud blows over a rover, it cleans off its solar panels. Both rovers continued to produce power for years longer than planned.

Stuck in the Sand

Spirit was a tough robot. In 2006, one of the rover's wheels jammed and stopped spinning. *Spirit* trekked on, now driving backward. As the wheel was dragged along, it churned up some of the Martian soil. To the scientists' delight, this soil revealed white silica dust. This compound may have been produced in hot springs when water was present on Mars. *Spirit* continued exploring for another three years until it became trapped in loose, sandy soil. NASA spent eight months trying to free the rover. But *Spirit* was stuck. The robot's mission was declared over in March 2011.

SPACE DISCOVERY

CONSIDERED A LUCKY FLUKE, AN ANALYSIS OF THE SOIL BENEATH THE SAND THAT *SPIRIT* DUG UP WHILE TRYING TO FREE ITSELF ALSO SHOWED EVIDENCE OF FORMER SURFACE WATER.

Opportunity

The *Opportunity* rover has outlived its twin, *Spirit*, by several years. *Opportunity* first touched down on the opposite side of Mars from its sibling on January 25, 2004. The landing site, a flat plain called Meridiani Planum, was chosen because a lot of **hematite**, a mineral that often forms in water, had been detected there by the *MGS*. This was where *Opportunity* would start its search for water.

Blueberries on Mars

Soon after landing, *Opportunity* came across small, round rocks that scientists nicknamed "blueberries." Some of the blueberries were lodged in the ground, while others were scattered loosely, like marbles. To analyze these spheres, *Opportunity* drove to an area that had a large amount of blueberries next to an area with few. After studying the rocks, the rover figured out that the balls were the source of the hematite the *MGS* had detected from above.

Meteors on Mars

Opportunity was the first robot to stumble across a **meteorite** on another planet. The space rock was found while the rover was traveling toward the heat shield it discarded on arrival in the Meridiani Planum. It was about the size of a basketball. After being analyzed by *Opportunity*, it was discovered that the meteorite was mostly made up of iron and nickel.

Three years into its mission, *Opportunity* arrived at Endeavour Crater. The crater is about 14 miles (22 km) wide. This was new ground for Martian exploration.

SPACE FIRST

Both *Spirit* and *Opportunity* were designed to travel about 1,968 feet (600 m) across the surface of Mars. Both rovers traveled much farther. *Spirit* explored a total distance of 4.8 miles (7.7 km). In March 2015, *Opportunity* set a record by becoming the first robot to complete a "marathon" on another planet. After 11 years and 2 months, the rover had trekked about 26.2 miles (42.2 km) across Mars's dusty surface.

Eagle Crater

Endurance Crater

Victoria Crater

Endeavour Crater

Marathon Valley

5 km

This aerial map plots *Opportunity's* travels across the Martian surface to Endeavour Crater.

The Phoenix Lander

Mars, like Earth, has an equator, or middle region, as well as a north and south pole. The Mars *Odyssey* orbiter, which was launched in 2001, had detected large amounts of ice below the planet surface near the north pole. The *Phoenix* lander was sent to explore this area in greater detail, reaching Mars on May 25, 2008.

The most important tool on *Phoenix* was its robotic arm. The arm measured just under 8 feet (2.3 m) long and could bend, like

This artist's picture shows *Phoenix*'s thrusters slowing its descent onto the planet's surface.

an elbow, in the middle. The arm was designed to move easily. It could go up and down, side to side, back and forth, and rotate. The arm was ready for anything and had a scoop for digging, a spade for scraping, and a file. A camera was attached to the elbow to give scientists a closeup look at the soil *Phoenix* dug up. Once a sample was scooped up, it was placed in the lander for analysis.

Frosty Findings

The lander made many important discoveries in the Martian Arctic. *Phoenix* confirmed the presence of ice at its landing site, which it melted during one experiment. It also tested the soil for **salinity**, and found moderate levels.

The *Phoenix* mission was planned to last three months, but the tough lander held out for five months. The lander was not designed to survive the harsh Martian winter. It was powered by solar energy and needed sunlight to recharge. NASA had hoped that the lander might awaken in the spring, but *Phoenix* stayed quiet. The lander sent its last message, "Triumph," to Earth on November 2, a fitting end to a successful mission to Mars.

SPACE FIRST

ON THE 99TH DAY OF ITS MISSION, *PHOENIX* OBSERVED SNOW FALLING ON MARS ABOUT 2.9 MILES (4 KM) AWAY FROM ITS LANDING SITE. THE SNOW DISAPPEARED BEFORE IT REACHED THE PLANET'S SURFACE.

Curiosity

Curiosity is the largest rover that has ever been sent to Mars. Its mission was to continue the search to figure out whether life has been, or is, present on Mars. Since 2011, *Curiosity* has been searching the red planet for clues to unlock the secrets of its past.

Daredevil Landing

Curiosity is a heavy-duty space robot, weighing 1 ton (0.9 mt). The robot's landing was nicknamed the "seven minutes of terror" by NASA. As *Curiosity* entered the Martian atmosphere, a parachute deployed. Thrusters then fired to slow *Curiosity*'s descent. *Curiosity* separated into two parts, and the sky crane part lowered the rover to the surface. When the computer sensed the rover had reached the surface, it cut the cord connecting it to the sky crane. Thrusters then fired at full blast to move the sky crane safely away from the landing site. *Curiosity* touched down in the bottom of Gale Crater.

Curiosity is powered by plutonium. This feeds the robot a constant stream of energy, so that it can operate day or night, and even on cloudy days.

Laser Power

Curiosity is packed with 10 scientific instruments. It is equipped with an extremely powerful laser, called the ChemCam, that beams out pulses of energy to blast rocks apart. Each pulse contains the same amount of energy it takes to power almost one million light bulbs. After each blast, the rover examines the rock to see what elements it is made of. This gives scientists clues as to how the planet formed.

An artist's concept shows *Curiosity's* laser blasting a rock to be tested in the rover's ChemCam.

Joyride

In August 2013, NASA placed *Curiosity* into autonomous drive mode. The rover set off, driving itself. *Curiosity* was able to analyze images of its surroundings for potential hazards, then determine the safest path to travel along. While the joyride only lasted for about 33 feet (10 m), this marked a huge step forward in showcasing robotic explorers' capacity for navigating and functioning by themselves.

SPACE FIRST

In 2012, *Curiosity* became the first rover to take a space "selfie" by extending its robotic arm and snapping several photos of itself. Like other rovers, *Curiosity* has its own Twitter feed that shares mission updates with millions of followers.

By far, NASA has been the most successful space agency to send robots to Mars. The former Soviet Union, the European Space Agency (ESA), and the Indian Space Research Organisation (IRSO) have launched other missions. These eyes in the sky give scientists the chance to examine all parts of the planet and zoom in on places of interest. Much of the research from orbiters has led to other robots being sent to the Mars's surface to investigate further.

Weather, Water, and Climate Change

The *MGS* reached Mars's orbit in September 1997. Its mission lasted four times longer than planned. Over its life, the *MGS* took more than 240,000 images and studied the planet's long-term weather. Findings from the orbiter suggested that the planet was experiencing climate change because ice deposits at the south pole shrank.

Mars *Odyssey*, which reached Mars in October 2004, was the first robotic spacecraft to detect frozen water on Mars. This led to the *Phoenix* lander mission.

Mars Express was planned as an orbiter-rover mission by the ESA. It launched in June, and arrived in December 2003. While the orbiter is still operational, the *Beagle* lander was lost on its way to the planet surface.

NASA's *Mars Reconnaissance* orbiter reached Mars on March 10, 2006. In 2015, NASA announced that the orbiter had detected salt water trickling down slopes in some places on Mars. Also that year, the orbiter spotted where *Beagle* had crash-landed more than 10 years earlier.

Talking to Earth and Mapping Mars

The *Mars Atmosphere and **Volatile** Evolution (MAVEN)* mission went into orbit above Mars in 2014, to examine the upper levels of the planet's atmosphere. *MAVEN* is powered by solar panels and uses a high-gain **antenna** to "talk" to scientists back on Earth twice a week. The spacecraft also acts as a switchboard, relaying messages back to mission control from *Curiosity* and *Opportunity*.

The *Mars Orbiter Mission (MOM)* was the first Indian spacecraft to reach Mars. The orbiter is mapping the surface of Mars to pave the way for future Indian space missions.

SPACE FIRST

THE *MAVEN* ORBITER DETECTED LIGHTS SIMILAR TO THE AURORA BOREALIS, OR NORTHERN LIGHTS, ON EARTH THAT LASTED FOR FIVE DAYS ACROSS MARS'S NORTHERN HEMISPHERE.

MAVEN records data from high above Mars.

Mission Failures

Despite many successes, there have been many more failures in the history of Mars exploration. Scientists study these missions to figure out what went wrong, and to make sure the same mistakes are not made on future missions.

Phobos 1 and *2* were two doomed spacecraft sent to Mars's largest moon, launched by the Soviet Union in 1988. Communication was lost with *Phobos 1* during the journey to Mars. *Phobos 2* made it into Mars's orbit, but as the spacecraft descended toward the surface of Phobos to release two landers, its onboard computer malfunctioned and lost contact.

NASA launched the *Mars Observer* orbiter on September 25, 1992. Just as the orbiter was nearing Mars, contact was lost. NASA also lost contact with the *Mars Climate* orbiter after the craft arrived at Mars in September 1999. Scientists believe that the orbiter got too close to the planet and burned up in the atmosphere.

The *Nozomi* orbiter was Japan's first shot at a mission to Mars. It launched on July 3, 1998. When *Nozomi* reached Mars, its thrusters failed to send the spacecraft into orbit. The craft flew past Mars and spent two years in an orbit around the sun.

Mars Polar Lander/Deep Space 2 was launched by NASA on January 3, 1999. Contact was lost with Earth when the lander reached Mars in December. Scientists are not sure what went wrong. Much of the technology aboard the *Polar Lander* made it to Mars with the later *Phoenix* mission.

Space First

Although *Viking 1* was the first successful landing on Mars, the first human-made object on the surface of Mars technically goes to the USSR's lander *Mars 2*, which crashed in 1971 during its descent.

This shows what the *Mars Polar Lander* may have looked like, had it been a successful mission.

InSight

A new robot is headed to Mars in 2016. Named *InSight* (*Interior Exploration using **Seismic** Investigations, **Geodesy**, and Heat Transport*), the lander's mission is to dig deep into Mars's geologic history to study how Mars and the other inner planets formed more than four billion years ago. The mission will examine the planet's core, crust, and mantle.

Mars is the perfect planet to study in order for scientists to learn about planet formation. Since Mars does not have as much geological activity as Earth, it has not changed as much as our home planet. By better understanding how Mars formed, scientists will learn more about how Mercury, Venus, and Earth were created, too.

Mission Goals

Much of *InSight*'s technology is based on the previous *Phoenix* lander. Unlike *Phoenix*, which landed at the north pole, the new lander is headed for a much warmer and sunnier location near the planet's equator. *InSight* is scheduled to launch in May, and land in September 2016. Its mission will last 708 sols, which is equal to 728 Earth days.

SPACE FIRST

THE *INSIGHT* MISSION WILL TAKE OFF FROM VANDENBERG AIR FORCE BASE NEAR LOS ANGELES, CALIFORNIA. THIS WILL BE THE FIRST TIME A NASA INTERPLANETARY MISSION HAS BLASTED OFF FROM ANYWHERE OTHER THAN CAPE CANAVERAL, FLORIDA.

Scientists hope to learn much about Mars's early evolution using technology on board *InSight*.

Measuring Mars

Like most robotic explorers, cameras will act as *InSight*'s eyes. The lander will also be fitted with three important tools to study the geology of Mars. A device called a seismometer measures earthquakes and other activity beneath the planet's surface. A heat probe, nicknamed "the mole," will drill down 16 feet (5 m) to take Mars's internal temperature. This will be the deepest hole any robotic explorer has dug on a planet other than Earth. The probe will measure how much heat is coming from the planet's core, which can tell scientists a lot about the planet's evolution. Another tool will measure how the sun's pull affects Mars. These measurements will teach scientists more about the building blocks inside the planet.

Future Missions to Mars

Hundreds of scientists and engineers are planning and designing more missions to the red planet. Here are some of the latest projects in the works for the next few years of exploration.

ExoMars

Several groups, including the ESA, NASA, and Roscosmos, Russia's space agency, are working together on the *ExoMars* mission. The mission is planned to take place in two stages: the launch of an orbiter followed by a rover. In March 2016, the orbiter will take off from the Baikonur Cosmodrome in Kazakhstan. The rover will

The *ExoMars* rover's solar panels will provide its main energy source.

follow two years later. The *ExoMars* rover will be the first robot to be able to move around the planet and dig in different locations. Its drill will be able to reach depths of up to 6 feet (2 m). The rover will then extract samples for analysis in its onboard laboratory. A spectrometer will test the rocks and soil found within the hole.

The ESA is using *ExoMars* as a stepping-stone to prepare for missions that will, one day, bring samples from Mars back to Earth for human scientists to study.

Mars 2020

NASA is planning to send a new rover to Mars in 2020, with a planned arrival of February 2021. The rover's launch and design will be based on the success of *Curiosity*. One key goal of the *Mars 2020* rover will be to make oxygen on Mars. Carbon dioxide makes up about 96 percent of the Martian atmosphere. A ground-breaking instrument called Mars Oxygen In-Situ Resources Utilization Experiment (MOXIE) will convert this carbon dioxide into oxygen and carbon monoxide. This technology could be crucial for providing an essential source of oxygen during human exploration.

SPACE FIRST

SCIENTISTS ARE ALWAYS THINKING ONE STEP AHEAD. THE MARS 2020 ROVER WILL BE THE FIRST NASA MISSION TO COLLECT SAMPLES FROM THE MARTIAN SURFACE. THESE WILL BE PLACED IN A SEALED CONTAINER TO BE BROUGHT BACK TO EARTH BY A FUTURE MISSION THAT IS NOT YET PLANNED.

The Next Giant Leap

The goal of many Mars missions has been to establish whether life has been, or could be, sustained on the planet. This was once only talked about in science fiction stories. Now, humans visiting the red planet could happen in the not-so-distant future.

Orion Spaceship

One of NASA's goals for the next generation of space travel is to send humans to Mars in the 2030s. To meet this goal, scientists and engineers are working hard on NASA's newest spacecraft. The ship, called *Orion*, is designed to take astronauts into deep space, and one day, to Mars. It will carry four passengers at a time. *Orion*'s first unmanned test-flight took place in December 2014. The flight was a success, making two orbits of Earth.

Humans on Mars

While robots can spend years alone on Mars, it is important for scientists to study the effect of long-term space travel on humans. In 2015, the HI-SEAS mission, short for Hawaii Space Exploration Analog and Simulation, finished an eight-month-long experiment, which placed six scientists in isolation on top of the Mauna Loa volcano in Hawaii. The volcanic surface is similar to what astronauts would encounter on Mars. The next isolation experiment is scheduled to last for one year. Any future missions to Mars will likely take between two-and-a-half and three years.

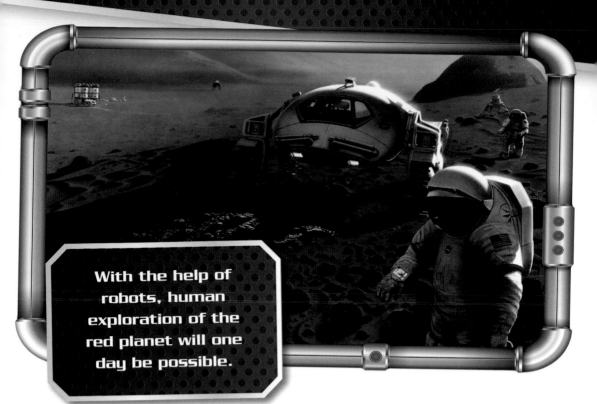

With the help of robots, human exploration of the red planet will one day be possible.

Mars One

Mars One's goal is to **terraform** the red planet. It plans to send two rovers to search for the best site for human settlement. The planned launch date for the rovers is 2020, with the first crew taking off six years later. Once on Mars, astronauts will wear spacesuits to protect against the planet's extreme temperatures and thin atmosphere. Then, finally, thanks to the work of the robots that went before them, humans will see the wonders of the red planet in person!

SPACE FIRST

MANY PEOPLE WANT TO BE AMONG THE FIRST TO SET FOOT ON MARS. IN 2015, OVER 2,000 PEOPLE APPLIED TO TAKE PART IN THE MARS ONE PROJECT FOR THE SEVEN-MONTH, ONE-WAY TRIP TO THE RED PLANET.

GLOSSARY

atmosphere A layer of gases that surround a planet or moon.

antenna Device for sending and receiving radio signals.

autonomously Independently from something else.

binary code A coding system that uses the numbers 0 and 1 to communicate a number, letter, or image to a computer.

element One of many basic substances that make up everything in the universe.

flybys When spacecraft fly close to a planet or moon in order to gain extra momentum from it.

geodesy A branch of mathematics that studies the size and shape of a planet as well as its gravitational field.

hematite A reddish-black mineral form of iron.

meteorite A rock or metal that has traveled through space and landed on a planet or moon.

mission control Scientists, technicians, and other people in charge of a space mission.

orbiting Traveling around an object in a circular way.

orbiters Spacecraft that travel through space, but do not land.

probes Robots that are programmed to explore a particular area of space.

salinity Describing the level of salt in something.

seismic Activity relating to an earthquake or other vibrations in the ground.

robots Machines that are programmed to carry out particular jobs.

sol A day on Mars.

solar panels Devices that convert the energy of sunlight into electricity.

terraform To transform another planet to support human life.

thrusters Small engines that are used to change the direction or speed of a spacecraft.

volatile Describing something that easily vaporizes.

FOR MORE INFORMATION

Books

Berger, Melvin, and Mary Kay Carson. *Discovering Mars: The Amazing Story of the Red Planet*. New York, NY: Scholastic, 2015.

Maxwell, Scott, and Catherine Chambers. *Mars Rover Driver* (The Coolest Jobs on the Planet). Mankato, MN: Heinemann, 2013.

O'Hearn, Michael. *Awesome Space Robots*. North Mankato, MN: Capstone Press, 2013.

Rusch, Elizabeth. *The Mighty Mars Rovers: The Incredible Adventures of* Spirit *and* Opportunity. New York, NY: HMH Books for Young Readers, 2012.

Websites

Due to the changing nature of Internet links, PowerKids Press has developed an online list of websites related to the subject of this book. This site is updated regularly. Please use this link to access the list: **www.powerkidslinks.com/res/mars**

INDEX